Knowing God's will

By

Pastor Rick Carter Jr. Ph.D.

Knowing God's Will

All Scripture taken from the authorized King James Bible

ISBN:

Table of Contents

“And he that searcheth the hearts knoweth what is the mind of the Spirit, because he maketh intercession for the saints according to the will of God.”

Romans 8:27

Chapter 1

Is there such a thing as God's will?

Is there such a thing as God's will? This may sound like a strange question to many, but it is a question that needs to be asked for several reasons. First, if there is a will of God for each individual, then it would be incumbent on every individual to know that and act upon it. Second, if there is a will of God and a person is not following it in their life, then they, by definition, would be out of God's will, and, we would assume, incur judgment for that disobedience. Knowing whether or not there is a will of God then becomes a very important area of concern.

To begin with let's define the term will. What is a will? The Webster's 1828 dictionary defines will as it relates to God as, "Divine determination; moral purpose or counsel." Based upon the Lord's model prayer in Matthew 6:10 which says, "Thy kingdom come. Thy will be done in earth, as it is in heaven." From a broad view the will is what we decide to do. The soul, made in the image of God, is made up of our intellect (how we think), our emotions (how we feel) and our volition or will (what we decide). Our decisions are generally based upon our thinking and feelings. When we speak of God's will, we are talking about those things that God has decided, and in context, we are talking about what things God has decided that He wants for our lives.

The Bible speaks often on the topic of God's will; as a matter of fact, there are at least 33 different passages in the New Testament that speak directly about the will of God in one fashion or another. In the verse referenced a moment ago from the Lord's model prayer, we are instructed to specifically pray for God's will to be done on this earth. If God's will did not impact this earth, or particularly us on this earth, then what would be the point in praying for God's will to be done? The truth is that this verse alone is sufficient to make the determination that there most certainly is such a thing as God's will, but let's not take just one verse as a proof. Consider the following things said about the will of God.

In Matthew 26:42, Jesus, during His prayer in the garden, submitted Himself to God's will for His crucifixion. In Matthew 7:21, Jesus taught that only those who do the will of God will enter into heaven. In Luke 12:47, Jesus taught that those who know their lord's will and refuse to prepare themselves for it or refuse to do it will suffer punishment. In Mark 3:35, Jesus says that those who do the will of God are His brothers and sisters. Certainly, we could conclude based upon scripture that Jesus believed there was such a thing as the will of God and not only that but that the will of God could be specific to an individual.

The teaching on the topic of God's will is not limited to just the teachings of Christ, though that should certainly be sufficient to put the question to rest. We also find the topic discussed by the apostles Paul, Peter, James, John, and the writer of Hebrews. In fact, the topic of God's will is addressed in 16 New Testament books directly. Paul talks repeatedly about the fact that he was called to be an apostle by the will of God. The entire book of 1 Peter is an address concerning submitting to God's will for our lives when we suffer for righteousness. The scope of the discussion on this topic in the Bible is broad and telling. There is just no way to deny, with any biblical credibility, that there is in fact such a thing as the will of God.

Having said that, we might ask that question that I am so frequently asked as a pastor, "How can I know the will of God for my life?" It is something that most believers struggle with at some point in their life if they are truly seeking to follow the Lord. The will of God is not something that God is trying to hide. Sometimes we act as though God's will is a hidden mystery that can only be found by a few; this is not how the Bible presents the topic. As a matter of fact, Paul tells us in Ephesians 5:17, "Wherefore be ye not unwise, but understanding what the will of the Lord is." It is safe to conclude from this verse that it is not only possible to know God's will, but it is also God's will for you to know His will.

Let's take a journey through the Bible in our next chapter and see the different ways which people have come to know the will of God in the scriptures. This will also answer some questions you may have about various methods that you have heard about in the past and whether they are a legitimate means of discerning God's will in your life.

Chapter 2

How hard is God's will to find?

There is a tendency to view finding God's will as an epic quest of legendary tale. Much like the allegorical tales of *The Pilgrim's Progress* or even fanciful tales such as the *Lord of the Rings,* some people think that they must accomplish great feats to find the hidden codes that reveal the secret key that unlocks the ancient book of the will of God. This is as fanciful as it sounds and is certainly not true in the slightest. Through the scriptures, we see God revealing His direct will to mankind in several ways.

In the beginning (I've always wanted to use that phrase in a book), God walked and talked with Adam and Eve in the garden in a personal way. They knew God's will because He verbally told them His will. There was no question of what God wanted them to do or not do. Let that sink in a bit because some might think that if they knew God's will, everything would suddenly change, they would become super-Christians and faithful servants. Even though Adam and Eve knew God's will, they still sinned in the Garden and caused the original fall of mankind." There is an alternate side to knowing God's will; if you are not willing to obey it then you are committing sin. It would appear that God spoke directly to mankind for some time even after their exile from the garden. God spoke to Cain in

Genesis chapter four and God spoke to Noah in Genesis chapter six. As a matter of fact, God spoke directly to select people all the way up through the patriarchs. Abraham heard directly from God on numerous occasions, Jacob wrestled with God physically and spoke to Him directly.
This direct verbal revelation seemed to end during the time Israel was in Egypt. It was at the calling of Moses that God, rather than giving individual direction to the patriarchs, began to speak through prophets and priests. Moses received direct communication from God and spoke to Him face to face. This might seem the same, but it began a point where God's will was revealed beyond the man himself. Unlike Noah and the patriarchs who heard directly from God, Moses was responsible for giving God's will to the people in an indirect way. Prophets proclaimed the will of God for the daily lives and decisions of the people. Yes, I know that Noah preached and gave warning of the impending flood, but, beyond the message of repentance, he was not concerned with anything other than obedience to the will of God revealed for his life in his preaching.

Moses, on the other hand, recorded God's will for how to deal with nearly every aspect of life. This was a vast change in the revelation of God's will since for the first time, the will of God was written down and access was made for any person to read and study it for themselves. The Pentateuch recorded the direct will of God for every person. This is what we would call the general will of God; it applied universally to all people. Before Moses, the written will of God was not delivered in such a way. Many believe that the book of Job may be the oldest book in the Bible and was possibly written by a contemporary of Abraham. Job himself says, however, that his greatest desire was that God would write His will down in a book so Job could read it (Job 31:35). Moses wrote that book, the revealed will of God for all mankind was expressed in his writing.

Throughout time, many more prophets would write out the will of God, primarily for the nation of Israel. Samuel, Nathan, Elijah, Elisha, Jeremiah, Isaiah, Ezekiel, Obadiah, Nahum, Jonah, Daniel, and we could go on, wrote out a revelation of God's will. It was not only prophets that were able to know the will of God however, God also began to reveal His will to priests.

One of the instructions that God gave to Moses was to make an Ephod with a breast plate that contained two stones called Urim and Thummim. Exactly what these stones are is debated but they were situated on the breast plate according to Exodus 28:30, "And thou shalt put in the breastplate of judgment the Urim and the Thummim; and they shall be upon Aaron's heart, when he goeth in before the LORD: and Aaron shall bear the judgment of the children of Israel upon his heart before the LORD continually." These stones were there for the priest to be able to determine the will of God when there was a question.

Numbers 27:21 explains it in this manner, "And he shall stand before Eleazar the priest, who shall ask counsel for him after the judgment of Urim before the LORD: at his word shall they go out, and at his word they shall come in, both he, and all the children of Israel with him, even all the congregation." The priest would ask a question and in some manner the stones would indicate an affirmative or negative answer. David received an ephod when one of the priests fled from Saul in 1 Samuel 23:6, "And it came to pass, when Abiathar the son of Ahimelech fled to David to Keilah, that he came down with an ephod in his hand." This began a new time for David, of being able through the priest and the working of God through the Ephod, to learn God's direct will for the choices he was making. David enquired often of God through the ephod to know God's will. Once such time is recorded in 1 Samuel 23:9-13, "And David knew that Saul secretly practised mischief against him; and he said to Abiathar the priest, Bring hither the ephod. Then said David, O LORD God of Israel, thy servant hath certainly heard that Saul seeketh to come to Keilah, to destroy the city for my sake. Will the men of Keilah deliver me up into his hand? will Saul come down, as thy servant hath heard? O LORD God of Israel, I beseech thee, tell thy servant. And the LORD said, He will come down. Then said David, Will the men of Keilah deliver me and my men into the hand of Saul? And the LORD said, They will deliver thee up. Then David and his men, which were about six hundred, arose and departed out of Keilah, and went whithersoever they could go. And it was told Saul that David was escaped from Keilah; and he forbare to go forth."

You can see here that David would ask a yes or no question, and in some manner, the Urim and Thummim would indicate an answer that revealed

God's will. It was not as expressive as the messages that God would send through the prophets, but it was distinct enough that a person was able to know the specific will of God for a situation. This, in some ways, created a distinction between the general will of God which the prophets delivered, the will of God for all the people and the specific will of God, the will of God for a select person.

Other men used the Ephod to determine the will of God and it didn't always turn out for them as they hoped. Gideon, who we will discuss again, also made an ephod but after he did the people began to worship the ephod rather than God, according to Judges 8:27 "And Gideon made an ephod thereof, and put it in his city, even in Ophrah: and all Israel went thither a whoring after it: which thing became a snare unto Gideon, and to his house." The people began to worship the ephod as if the ephod was God, rather than recognizing that God was speaking to them through the ephod in a limited manner. This is often the danger of such things if people's hearts are not right with God. As a matter of fact, God stopped speaking through every means to Saul because his heart was not right according to 1 Samuel 28:6, "And when Saul enquired of the LORD, the LORD answered him not, neither by dreams, nor by Urim, nor by prophets."

The Bible tells us that there will again be a priest that will use the ephod again in Ezra 2:63 "And the Tirshatha said unto them, that they should not eat of the most holy things, till there stood up a priest with Urim and with Thummim." Israel will again hear from

God in a direct manner at some point as He begins to draw them back to Himself.

There are a few other methods of God revealing His will in the Old Testament that I think we should mention. One is through dreams. We see this take place extensively in the life of Joseph, but he was not the only one. This first takes place with Abimelech, as God gives him a warning. God spoke to Jacob in a dream. He also spoke to the Egyptian butler, baker and Pharaoh in dreams. As well as Solomon, Daniel and Nebuchadnezzar. I have often heard people speak of God talking to them in dreams, and I cannot tell you that He never does this anymore, but I can share with you a warning that God gives to Israel in Deuteronomy 13:1-5, "If there arise among you a prophet, or a dreamer of dreams, and giveth thee a sign or a wonder, And the sign or the wonder come to pass, whereof he spake unto thee, saying, Let us go after other gods, which thou hast not known, and let us serve them; Thou shalt not hearken unto the words of that prophet, or that dreamer of dreams: for the LORD your God proveth you, to know whether ye love the LORD your God with all your heart and with all your soul. Ye shall walk after the LORD your God, and fear him, and keep his commandments, and obey his voice, and ye shall serve him, and cleave unto him. And that prophet, or that dreamer of dreams, shall be put to death; because he hath spoken to turn you away from the LORD your God, which brought you out of the land of Egypt, and redeemed you out of the house of bondage, to thrust thee out of the way which the LORD thy God commanded thee to walk in. So shalt thou put the evil away from the midst of thee." To summarize what I see in this passage, let's say, be extremely careful about using dreams to determine the will of God. It is highly likely that you are being tested and you should seek to the Bible to make sure you don't get messed up.

We also see God, at times, revealing His will to people in the Old Testament through angels. God sent an angel to divert and speak to Balaam, Abraham, Lot and others. The revealed will of God in these circumstances was always very specific to the individual. In this manner, God told Balaam not to curse Israel, Abraham that he would have a son, Lot to leave Sodom and so on. An angelic messenger delivered revelation to Daniel, and in the New Testament we know that angels were used by God to speak to several including Zacharias, Joseph and Mary, Jesus, Philip, Cornelius, Peter, Paul and John. That is quite a list of people in the New Testament that God spoke to through an angel and there are many more we could list in the Old Testament. I have often been asked, "does God still speak to people through angels?" While much like the question of dreams, I cannot dogmatically say He will not (He can do whatever He wants, He is God after all). I will say that I would be highly suspicious of someone telling me that an angel came and revealed God's will to them for two reasons. First, Paul warns us in 2 Corinthians 11:14, "And no marvel; for Satan himself is transformed into an angel of light." Satanic spirits can appear to be angels and in so doing deceive people. John warns about this as well in 1 John 4:1, "Beloved, believe not every spirit, but try the spirits whether they are of God: because many false prophets are gone out into the world." John even gives us a test that can be used to try a spirit in such a situation that a person might believe they have been spoken to in the following verses. 1 John 4:2 "Hereby know ye the Spirit of God: Every spirit that confesseth that Jesus Christ is come in the flesh is of God: And every spirit that confesseth not that Jesus Christ is come in the flesh is not of God: and this is that spirit of antichrist, whereof ye have heard that it should come; and even now already is it in the world." If a Spirit cannot confess that Jesus Christ is come in the flesh, then they are not of God. I don't mean they can say yes or no to that question, but rather that they will confess it verbally or refuse to.

Now it might be improbable that you will ever have a spirit speak to you but, should that ever occur, remember this test that John gives us. Another important way to determine if it is of God is to compare whatever you have heard to the Scriptures and make sure that it is in direct alignment with God's Word. God will never lead a person contrary to what He has already delivered to us in the Bible. The devil, on the other hand, will twist and pervert the scripture. Remember when Satan tempted Eve, he used parts of God's Words. And he did the same with Christ. So just because someone or some spirit seems to be quoting the Bible doesn't mean they are quoting it right or that the way they are using it is in line with the context of the scriptures. All such communication should be highly examined. And I would also warn that no person should ever seek out such communication at all. If God wants to speak, He knows where you are. You seek

Him in His revealed Word and not through attempting to contact spirits or you will be in great danger of interaction with the wrong kind of spirit, as Saul did.

Another method, of God revealing His will in the Old Testament, is through miraculous manifestation, such as causing Balaam's donkey to speak or giant handwriting on the wall. I am referring here to the way God spoke to Belteshazzar in Daniel 5:5, "In the same hour came forth fingers of a man's hand, and wrote over against the candlestick upon the plaister of the wall of the king's palace: and the king saw the part of the hand that wrote." Many believers today would like for God to speak to them in this or the last way we have discussed. They want to see some angelic being or some miraculous event take place so that they could know God's will. But I submit to you that knowing the will of God does not take these things. In the case of Belteshazzar, God was giving him a warning and if you must have a warning like this to know God's will, then you probably don't want to know what God thinks.

A final method we see in the scriptures, which seems to be popular even to practice today, is what we see Gideon do when he put out a fleece in Judges 6:36 -40 "And Gideon said unto God, If thou wilt save Israel by mine hand, as thou hast said, Behold, I will put a fleece of wool in the floor; and if the dew be on the fleece only, and it be dry upon all the earth beside, then shall I know that thou wilt save Israel by mine hand, as thou hast said. And it was so: for he rose up early on the morrow, and thrust the fleece together, and wringed the dew out of the fleece, a bowl full of water. And

Gideon said unto God, Let not thine anger be hot against me, and I will speak but this once: let me prove, I pray thee, but this once with the fleece; let it now be dry only upon the fleece, and upon all the ground let there be dew. And God did so that night: for it was dry upon the fleece only, and there was dew on all the ground."

I have heard so many people talk about putting fleeces before God to determine God's will for their lives. I want to point out a few inconsistent facts about this, however. First, Gideon already knew God's will. He had been told directly by an angel what God wanted him to do, so putting out the fleece had nothing to do with learning God's will. The fleece was something Gideon did to ask God to give him a sign that God was with him as he went forward to do what he had been asked. The idea that I have heard so many use this to express, is that they put out a few ideas before God and said God if you want me to go this way do this and if you want me to go that way do another thing. This is not what Gideon was doing at all. The second issue I have with this is that it isn't as though we see this happen anywhere in the New Testament. There are no fleeces put out by the apostles, there is no verse that instructs us to put out fleeces to know God's will at all.

We don't see this as an endorsed method anywhere in the New Testament. Yet, it is so often employed by Christians in our day and I fail to see the reason for that. Gideon was not trying to find the will of God; he was trying to find the confidence to do the will of God that he already knew. I would submit to you that this method of trying to find God's will is easily manipulated since we are using circumstances to determine the will of God and we know quite well in scripture that Satan can affect circumstances just as he did when afflicting Job. We are even warned in 2 Corinthians 11:13-15, "For such are false apostles, deceitful workers, transforming themselves into the apostles of Christ. And no marvel; for Satan himself is transformed into an angel of light. Therefore it is no great thing if his ministers also be transformed as the ministers of righteousness; whose end shall be according to their works." Then we are told in 2 Thessalonians 2:9 "Even him, whose coming is after the working of Satan with all power and signs and lying wonders," So if Satan and his workers can transform themselves to seem as God's ministers and do signs and lying wonders, what makes you think that they cannot accomplish fulfilling a fleece? As a matter of fact, during the tribulation, we know that the devil will do such amazing physical miracles that people will believe he is God.

In the New Testament we do see God revealing His will a few times by means of dreams and angelic visitation. We more prominently see that God's will is revealed by the indwelling Holy Spirit, which none of the Old Testament writers had the privilege of knowing in the way that we do as New Testament Believers, and by the completed Word of God, which was also not available to anyone in the Old Testament. I would submit to you that it is by these two avenues that God primarily works today. As a matter of fact, if you are walking in the Word and in fellowship with the Spirit, there is no need for God to work in any other way. We see this transition take place throughout the New Testament so that by the end of the New Testament we read primarily of the direction of the Holy Spirit through the Word of God in the life of the believer. In the next few chapters, we will explore this in much more detail so that it will be easy to understand.

Chapter 3

The general will of God

God's will can be divided broadly into two categories: 1. God's general will for all people. 2. God's specific will for your life. These two areas will give us a break down to consider the will of God for the next few chapters.

Romans 12:1-2 "I beseech you therefore, brethren, by the mercies of God, that ye present your bodies a living sacrifice, holy, acceptable unto God, which is your reasonable service. And be not conformed to this world: but be ye transformed by the renewing of your mind, that ye may prove what is that good, and acceptable, and perfect, will of God."

Romans 12 begins a discussion on the gifts of the Spirit to believers for serving and it lays the groundwork for what is necessary in order to use the gifts that God has given to you. Verse one declares the need for surrender to God. You will never accomplish God's will until you put your will down. You must sacrifice your body to God in a living way, rejecting the desire to fulfill your lusts and instead live a holy life. It is only reasonable that a believer would do this since Christ has laid down His life for us that we might be saved. In doing this, we will reject conforming to this present evil world, and we will be transformed into the image of Christ by renewing our mind and following the direction of God. In following God's direction, we see an interesting statement concerning the will of God. The will of God, here in Romans 12:2, is divided into the good, acceptable and the perfect.

I believe that the good will of God is what could also be called the general will of God. The general will of God is what is good for everyone. There is no one who falls outside the scope of God's good will for all men. Let me illustrate with some Biblical examples. It tells us in 2 Peter 3:9, "The Lord is not slack concerning his promise, as some men count slackness; but is longsuffering to us-ward, not willing that any should perish, but that all should come to repentance." Here we find a two-fold explanation of God's will for all people. First, we see that it is not God's will that any should perish. In other words, it is against the will of God that anyone would die and go to hell. Instead, God's will is that everyone would repent and by doing so would be saved. Anyone that goes to hell does so against the will of God.

There is a false doctrine that has been taught concerning the sovereignty of God and the free will of man. This false idea is that if man has a free will to choose salvation, then this somehow negates the sovereignty of God. The fact that this is a false idea is evident in the very inception of the Bible when God placed Adam and Eve in the garden and commanded them not to eat of the tree of the knowledge of good and evil. God gave man a free will to choose good and evil from the very beginning. Just as they had freedom to choose fellowship with God over disobedience, we have the freedom to choose fellowship with God through Christ Jesus. And it is the good will of God that everyone would choose this. But God does not force His will on mankind. God shares His will with us and allows us to choose. This in no way negates the fact that God in His sovereignty has ordained that our choice to receive or reject His offer of salvation would have eternal consequences. You can choose to reject Christ, but the sovereignty of God determined that if you do so you will spend eternity in Hell. This is how the sovereignty of God interacts with the free will of man; He doesn't force us to accept Christ, but we must suffer the consequences if we reject Him. People are allowed to make the choice, but they are not allowed to determine the consequences. The sovereignty of God has already done that.

The good will of God goes beyond salvation. It is also God's will for every believer to follow Christ in baptism. This is clear in the great commission that Jesus Christ gave to the Church that He established. It tells us in Matthew 28:19, "Go ye therefore, and teach all nations, baptizing them in the name of the Father, and of the Son, and of the Holy Ghost:" Everyone in the New Testament that received Christ was baptized in obedience to this command. For a person to be in the good will of God for all people today, they should receive Christ and be scripturally baptized.

We know from Acts 2:41, "Then they that gladly received his word were baptized: and the same day there were added unto them about three thousand souls." We see here God's will for spiritual progression revealed: salvation (receiving the Word), baptism and then being added to them (the New Testament Church). The vast majority of New Testament writing was to churches as opposed to individuals. God's desire is for His children to be under the authority and protection of His local, visible assemblies where we can worship, fellowship, study and serve.

It is the good will of God to read and study the Bible. 2 Timothy 2:15 says "Study to shew thyself approved unto God, a workman that needeth not to be ashamed, rightly dividing the word of truth." A believer who is not reading and studying the Word of God regularly, is not walking in the good will of God. How can you know the Lord as you ought or receive direction from Him, if you are not in His revealed Word? I know in my own life, that when I fail to spend time in God's Word daily, I begin to fall to fleshly thinking. Maintaining a spiritual thinking process requires faithfulness in God's Word in my life. I don't believe that is unique to me. I have spent far too many hours counseling and ministering to people to accept that there is any person on this earth that can abstain from regular daily time in God's Word and still be truly spiritually minded. The problem is that our pride convinces us that we are spiritual without God. The lie of the devil deceives us to the point that we believe that our natural thoughts are spiritual and since we are not in God's Word we are never confronted on that lie.

It is the good will of God for a believer to pray continually. 1 Thessalonians 5:17 says "Pray without ceasing." Surveys indicate that the average Christian prays no more than 15 minutes a day. That is 1,425 minutes short of God's instruction for prayer time. God wants to hear from us and speak to us continually, but our heart must be kept in the right place in order for that to happen. Of course, there is a difference between the closet prayer life that we are to have and the "without ceasing" attitude of prayer that we are to maintain. Unfortunately, we often switch prayer on and off and spend most of our time in the carnal mind. A prayer without ceasing attitude seeks God's will in every situation and decision.

In addition to these things, we know it to be God's will for every believer to grow in holiness. We are told in Romans 6:19, "I speak after the manner of men because of the infirmity of your flesh: for as ye have yielded your members servants to uncleanness and to iniquity unto iniquity; even so now yield your members servants to righteousness unto holiness." Over and again we are told to put on holiness; this is the idea of yielding yourself to the sanctifying work of the Holy Spirit in you. As He speaks to you through His Word and prayer, He will indicate those things that hinder us from walking closer to Him. It seems that some in our day have adopted a wrong idea of liberty in Christ that teaches that since we are under grace, we are at liberty to live according to the flesh. This could not be further from God's will. We are at liberty from sin, not to sin. This could not be clearer than Paul states in Galatians 5:13 "For, brethren, ye have been called unto liberty; only use not liberty for an occasion to the flesh, but by love serve one another." Paul calls this sanctification and if you still doubt whether it is God's will for you to yield yourself to it, then consider what He says in 1 Thessalonians 4:3, "For this is the will of God, even your sanctification, that ye should abstain from fornication:"

There are many other things that are contained in the general will of God for every believer, such as thankfulness (1 Thessalonians 5:18, "In every thing give thanks: for this is the will of God in Christ Jesus concerning you."), good works (1 Peter 2:15, "For so is the will of God, that with well doing ye may put to silence the ignorance of foolish men:") and enduring suffering (1 Peter 4:19, "Wherefore let them that suffer according to the will of God commit the keeping of their souls to him in well doing, as unto a faithful Creator."). These and many other things fall under the general will of God and show us why it is important to study to show ourselves approved to God. You don't have to be a pastor or full-time Christian worker to learn and obey the general good will of God; every believer is responsible to these things and should take them very seriously if they love God.

Obedience to the good will of God is, however, a daily decision. No one is standing as a watchman over your daily decisions. You have to choose to be obedient to Christ on your own. The motivation for this obedience should not be worry for judgment. I have talked to so many people who spent all their time in a fleshly fear of the judgment of God should they forget or fail to do something. The Bible certainly speaks of the necessity of the fear of the Lord and while there is certainly an aspect of this fear that implies a concern of judgment, there is a greater portion of it that simply means to reverence (show respect and admiration) to God. A young child may be motivated by fear of discipline, but it is far better if they learn to obey because of the fear of reverence. Often the fear of the Lord simply can mean that you have chosen to see things from God's perspective and accept His view as that which is true on any topic.

Beyond the fear of the Lord, there is no doubt that the greatest motivation for a believer should be love for God. If we love Him as we ought, then obedience to His will and conformity to His commandments is not a burden. When we look at the law, we see two primary purposes. One of these has to do with our relationship to the law before our conversion. Paul says in Galatians 3:24-25, "Wherefore the law was our schoolmaster to bring us unto Christ, that we might be justified by faith. But after that faith is come, we are no longer under a schoolmaster." Before salvation, the law shows us our need for Christ our Savior. After we are saved, though we are not any longer under our school master, this doesn't mean that suddenly the law is of no value to us, however. When I was in school, I was under the law of the answer key and it ruled what grade I received. After I left school, however, the right answers were still of a great value to me. As a matter of fact they often became of more value to me. Getting an A on my math test seems far less important now than keeping a correct balance in my check book. I am not under the law of the answer key, but I still use the same truths daily.

Now that we are not under the condemnation of the law, we are free to live according to the greater purpose of the law. That is to be a guide for how to love. When questioned about the greatest commandment, Jesus answered in Matthew 22:37-40, "Jesus said unto him, Thou shalt love the Lord thy God with all thy heart, and with all thy soul, and with all thy mind. This is the first and great commandment. And the second is like unto it, Thou shalt love thy neighbour as thyself. On these two commandments hang all the law and the prophets." The greatest commandment was not a single commandment but a summary of the commandments from God's perspective. The summary was that the commandments were to teach us how to love. When viewed from this idea, all the commandments become positive since they are instruction on how to show love. If I love God, I will put Him first in my life without exception, I will worship Him alone, I will praise Him and never blaspheme, and I will keep holy those things that He has said are holy. If I love others, I will honor authority (your parents are the first authority), life, marriage, property and truth and I will subdue my lusts. This is the ten commandments from a view of love.

Paul warns us about the issue of lusts, however, and how they impact the commandments when he says in Romans 7:7 "What shall we say then? Is the law sin? God forbid. Nay, I had not known sin, but by the law: for I had not known lust, except the law had said, Thou shalt not covet." To covet is to give into your lusts. If you view the commandments from this side, you find them to all be a hinderance to the fulfilment of your desires. You will lie to get what you want, you will steal, live in perversion, kill, disobey authority, violate the holy, blaspheme, commit idolatry, and put yourself ahead of God. If you view the commandments from love, they are all a means to demonstrate it; if you view the commandments from lust, they are all an obstacle to fulfilment.

To abide in the good will of God, you must keep love as your motive. 1 Timothy1:5 says "Now the end of the commandment is charity out of a pure heart, and of a good conscience, and of faith unfeigned:" We could say it like this, the goal of the commandments is to bring you to a point where you show love out of a pure heart. God's love perfected in us will produce this without any burden. We are told this very thing in 1 John 5:2-3, "By this we know that we love the children of God, when we love God, and keep his commandments. For this is the love of God, that we keep his commandments: and his commandments are not grievous." The good will of God will lead every person to this place of love for Him and their neighbor.

Chapter 4

The specific will of God

Having considered the general will of God, let's now turn our attention to the specific will of God. This as well is addressed in Romans 12:1-2, "I beseech you therefore, brethren, by the mercies of God, that ye present your bodies a living sacrifice, holy, acceptable unto God, which is your reasonable service. And be not conformed to this world: but be ye transformed by the renewing of your mind, that ye may prove what is that good, and acceptable, and perfect, will of God." Here, the specific will of God is divided into two parts, God's perfect will and His acceptable will. The specific will of God is what most people are speaking about when they say they are looking for God's will in their lives. This has to do with the details of the decisions and direction of your life. How does God want you to serve, where does He want you to live, work and so on. The specific will of God may have many parts for you, and you should seek to know the details of that.

Some would say that God will forgive the where if you will do the what. What they meant is that as long as you go soul-winning then God will allow you to do it anywhere you like without consequence. The ironic thing about that is that many times the same people will tell you that they have received the call of God directing them to a specific place. If the first statement was true, then the latter statement is strange. Why did God bother to direct them to a specific place if the place was unimportant and God would have forgiven them if they stayed where they were? The reality is that both the what and where are part of God's specific will and both are important. A failure to yield to the what will put you out of God's will all together, a failure to yield to the where may do the same, or it could move you from the perfect to the acceptable will of God. The pastor in question was really saying that it is ok to be in the acceptable will of God doing the what and miss the perfect will of God following the where. This is not good advice for anyone.

The perfect will of God carries with it a special promise of blessing. When God called Israel out of the bondage of Egypt, He also gave them a direction to go to the promised land. They left Egypt, they received the law at Mount Sinai, they experienced the power of God through the plagues, the crossing of the red sea, they saw the pillar of cloud by day and fire by night, they knew the reality of fellowship with God by seeing his face glow after being in God's presence. God instructed them to enter the promised land and they balked. They allowed their own fears to hold them back and they said no to the perfect will of God. They had been in the wilderness up to this point and while there they were in the perfect will of God. Once they refused God's further instruction, they were no longer in the perfect will of God, but they did not go back to Egypt. They stayed in the wilderness. Going back to Egypt would have certainly taken them out of the will of God. Staying in the wilderness prevented them from being in the perfect will of God. Once they realized this, they changed their minds, they said ok, we will go in then, but it was too late. God told them that they could not go in until the generation that had refused died away. They were prevented from going forward, but they could also not go back. They wandered in the wilderness for forty years. There in the wilderness they still had the provision of God with water from the rock and manna from heaven, they still had the protection of God as He defended them, and they still had the presence of God He still spoke to them through Moses. Yet they missed out on the promise of God, they had meager blessings and lacked abundant fulfillment. The wilderness was the acceptable will of God because they rejected the perfect will of God.

The perfect will of God is full of promise and blessings. Yes, there would have still been battles but the battle is different than struggle in the wilderness. In the perfect will of God, the enemy is primarily before you. You can see them, and God has promised to fight them for you. In the wilderness, however, the enemy is primarily within you. It is your own lusts and discontentment that destroys you the most. It was murmuring and complaining that brought the judgment of God on them in the wilderness, it was discontentment with authority and provision that plagued them in the wilderness. We don't see these things to the same extent in the promised land.

Let me offer some more personal input on this for a moment. I was called to preach at seventeen years old. By nineteen, I was married and had started a church.

God blessed that work immensely, within six months He had given us a building debt free and we had seen folks get saved and baptized. The church was doing well when I was encouraged by another pastor to leave there and come to be a church planter out of his church. He was a good man and well meaning, but it was not God's perfect will for us. I missed that in my youth; I was flattered that someone wanted me to come be their church planter, they made us promises and it seemed as though the circumstances all made sense. I resigned and found a man to come take the work so we could move and engage in our next church plant. Things didn't quite work like we had believed they would. I don't blame that pastor, as I said he was a good man, I blame myself for not being more in tune to the perfect will of God in my life. God even sent a faithful servant to warn me, a wonderful friend who instead of listening to him, I got angry with him.

We moved and started up the next church. We still had people get saved and we still saw God use us, we were doing the what and God was indeed blessing His Word, but the blessings in our lives personally had dried up. We were failing of many of the graces of God that we needed, and we were falling further away from the closeness that we had with God in the first work. After three years and much struggle we were on the verge of catastrophe. Our marriage was in trouble and our ministry was in trouble. We had thought we would be moving where we would have so much more help and yet we felt more alone than we ever had. We had moved from the perfect will to the acceptable will of God. It was a deceptive time because God has promised His Word will not return void, so we interpreted God blessing His Word as God blessing us. But it wasn't the same and we knew it.

Then one day I received a call from another pastor. He told me he would like to take me to lunch. I went with excitement, believing that things were finally going to turn around and we would be able to have the fellowship that we longed for. My disappointment was staggering when I sat down for lunch to hear him say, "Brother Carter, let me get right to it. God has told me to come and pastor in the town you are in so I am just wanting to ask when you are going to resign so I can become the pastor." If you were surprised, imagine how I felt! I was kind but inwardly appalled that he had the audacity to approach me like that. I went home and told my wife and we were both angry for a few days. Then a light bulb came on. We sat down and talked about how unhappy we were, how out of touch with God we were and how things had been before in our lives. We stopped and we prayed, something we hadn't been doing. I know that you might be surprised to hear this, but there are many who are in the work of God who spend significant time not walking with God. In truth, I was studying to preach only, I was not walking with God, I had allowed sin into my life and I was, for all practical purposes, on my way completely out of God's will.

We prayed, we started having personal devotions again, we started seeking God's face and, in a few days, we knew that God wanted us to leave. Let me be clear, it wasn't the circumstance that told us God's will, but

God did smack us in the head with the circumstance. As we sought God, He directed us to move to Oklahoma City and attend Beth Haven Baptist Seminary. We went through the process of resigning, the other preacher came to candidate, the church called him and then he said, let me pray about it. By that time, we had gotten to that point we had already enrolled in school, resigned our jobs, scheduled our move and were two weeks away from our move. The week before we left, he called to say that he had misunderstood God and wasn't going to come after all. We were faced with a quandary. Do we go according to what God had made clear in our hearts by seeking His face or do we stay because of the circumstances? We knew what it was like not being in God's perfect will, so we took several days to make sure we knew God's direction and we went ahead and moved. We sought to continue helping the church find a pastor even after we left but we left to pursue the perfect will of God.

Once we got to Oklahoma, we faced trials immediately. We were three months without utilities in our house, the job we thought we had lined up fell through and I couldn't find a job that paid enough to make it. We joined the church and found out that it would be six months before we could do anything at all after pastoring for over five years. Through all this, there was the temptation to move back and stay in the wilderness so to speak. It was certainly more comfortable in the wilderness at the time, but the will of God wasn't to stay there. Two months after our move, when we were in the worst of the transition, we got a call from one of the men of the church we had resigned, who begged us to return. You don't know how much we longed to go back, but we had confidence in our hearts that we were in the will of God for the first time in several years and being in God's perfect will was more important than being comfortable to us.

A few weeks after that call, it was as though God flipped a switch. He gave me a great job, we started learning things that helped our marriage and all of a sudden the struggle changed to joy. I have found that very often when someone is in the acceptable will of God, they will begin to let sin creep into their lives. Complacency and discontentment will be major problems for them. When they seek to move from the acceptable to the perfect will of God, they will face major opposition in their lives. I believe this is God's proving process for us. It is so easy to get out of the perfect will of God, but it is not as easy to get back into it. The first thing they found, as they crossed the Jordan river to enter the promised land, was a battle. It seemed impossible that they could conquer a city as fortified as Jericho and yet they followed God's will and He won the battle. This proving time is needed to make sure that we are serious about God's perfect will, to see if we have learned the lessons from our exile in the wilderness.

I don't believe that you should allow yourself to be paralyzed by fear of not being in God's perfect will, but I do believe that it is vital that you learn how to know the voice of God in your heart so that you can follow when He directs. We will talk more about that in the coming chapters. Suffice it to say that the blessings of being in the perfect will of God are so much better than the meager provision of the acceptable will of God. If, as you have read this so far, you find yourself in the acceptable rather than the perfect will of God, I challenge you to get yourself back in God's good will and begin to seek His face to give you the opportunity to return to His perfect will. Wait for Him to do it, don't try to move without His direction or you may continue in the wrong. If you seek Him, you will find Him, and you can know the power of the blessings from being in His perfect will.

Chapter 5

Moving past feelings and circumstances

Over many years of pastoring, I have heard all kinds of explanations invoking the will of God for people's lives that defy Biblical truth. I have heard the "I just feel" line so often and I have yet to believe that it is a suitable justification for making life-altering decisions. Much of the time when people come into my counseling office, they have already made up their minds about what they are going to do based upon how they feel and their reading of the circumstances. As if finding the will of God was like reading tea leaves or tarot cards. We look at the circumstances and say, "based upon my interpretation of these factors I believe God wants me to...", the problem here is that we don't find such direction in the Bible. As a matter of fact, we find a vastly different view when we consider the Biblical narrative.

If Peter and John would have been looking at the circumstances of being beaten and cast into prison in Acts 5, they would have stopped preaching. If Stephen would have considered the previous circumstances, he would have never preached in Acts 7. And what of the fact that he was stoned, wouldn't those circumstances discourage others from preaching publicly as he did? As a matter of fact, all through the book of Acts, we see nothing but negative circumstances. Abuse, prison, death and torture litter the trail of the apostles and early church, what part of those circumstances were they to use to determine the will of God?

I say all that because we use circumstances in a specific way to decide what God wants most of the time. If things are good, then it must be God's will because God wants what is good and if things are bad, then it must not be God's will since God could never want us to experience bad things. Doesn't this fly in the face of the very account of Scripture? Can you imagine Paul saying to Timothy, "Just follow your feelings and weigh the circumstances to decide what to do." Of course that sounds absurd, but that is what so many believers today do and then call it the will of God. This is as far from finding the will of God as you can possibly get.

Consider this example from the life of Paul found in Acts 14:19-23, "And there came thither certain Jews from Antioch and Iconium, who persuaded the people, and, having stoned Paul, drew him out of the city, supposing he had been dead. Howbeit, as the disciples stood round about him, he rose up, and came into the city: and the next day he departed with Barnabas to Derbe. And when they had preached the gospel to that city, and had taught many, they returned again to Lystra, and to Iconium, and Antioch, Confirming the souls of the disciples, and exhorting them to continue in the faith, and that we must through much tribulation enter into the kingdom of God. And when they had ordained them elders in every church, and had prayed with fasting, they commended them to the Lord, on whom they believed."

If Paul had been following the feelings and circumstances method of finding God's will, he would certainly not have returned to the city where he had just been stoned. I find it hard to believe that he felt much like doing much after being stoned and left for dead. Yet he got up and went right back to work doing what he had been called to do. Why? Because how he felt and the circumstances were not what determined the will of God in his life. He knew the will of God in a far deeper way than just the surface of feelings.

When the will of God becomes about feelings and circumstances, it becomes very shallow. In this manner, people will shift what they think of the will of God day to day or even faster. Circumstances and feelings can change quickly, but the will of God is steadfast. The will of God is not based upon the shifting sands of this world. God has called us to change this world, not be carried along with it. It tells us in James 1:5-8, "If any of you lack wisdom, let him ask of God, that giveth to all men liberally, and upbraideth not; and it shall be given him. But let him ask in faith, nothing wavering. For he that wavereth is like a wave of the sea driven with the wind and tossed. For let not that man think that he shall receive any thing of the Lord. A double minded man is unstable in all his ways." Far too many believers are driven with the winds of feelings and changing circumstances; they become double minded about the will of God. I have seen people switch churches, ministries, and even marriages, based upon what they were reading in the circumstances and trying to define that as the changing will of God. God is not that fickle!

In 2 Corinthians 8:5, we learn that the Macedonian churches, in spite of their deep poverty, gave not considering their own circumstances when Paul says, "And this they did, not as we hoped, but first gave their own selves to the Lord, and unto us by the will of God." Feelings and circumstances have caused many to withhold what they had rather than giving because they didn't recognize the leadership of the Holy Spirit and let their fears overcome His leadership. Feelings and circumstances are most often influenced by fears and lusts rather than by the foundation of scripture.

It tells us in Hebrews 10:36, "For ye have need of patience, that, after ye have done the will of God, ye might receive the promise." By this, we know that often doing the will of God will not seem to line up with the circumstances and we must have a patient dependence on the Lord to wait for the fulfillment of His promise that accompanies His will. You cannot experience this promise if you are constantly analyzing your feelings and looking at circumstances. The will of God must come from a far more secure knowing in your spirit that is confirmed by the presence of the Holy Ghost. It must be that the will of God is sought out in Spirit and in truth rather than on the shifting waves of this world. We must do as James 1:4 tells us and "let patience have her perfect work, that ye may be perfect and entire, wanting nothing."

Paul tells us in Romans 8:14, "For as many as are led by the Spirit of God, they are the sons of God. For ye have not received the spirit of bondage again to fear; but ye have received the Spirit of adoption, whereby we cry, Abba, Father. The Spirit itself beareth witness with our spirit, that we are the children of God: And if children, then heirs; heirs of God, and joint-heirs with Christ; if so be that we suffer with him, that we may be also glorified together." God wants you to know the deep fellowship of His Spirit that will show you the mind of Christ. His Spirit wants to bear witness with your spirit concerning His presence and His will. So many remain in the shallows of the faith, constantly watching the winds and waves rather than walking with Christ on the waters by faith. The constant consideration of the storm that rages around you and your fears that swell in your heart are no way to navigate the will of God. They are not dependable, and they are not useful to knowing what God really wants for you.

Can you not see Peter, his eyes fixed on the eyes of our Savior, stepping out of the boat without a care in this world, certain that the will of God was for Him to follow in the footsteps of Christ? He was in the perfect will of God to do so. Jesus had bid him to come and there he was walking on the water, doing the impossible with all the other disciples amazed that he would go against the circumstances and feelings that they all saw and had. It was short-lived, though, wasn't it? He forgot that his usual method of determining God's will was by sight, so he returned to it only to find himself sinking in the circumstances. In his fear, he cried out and Jesus reached out and saved him. What I am saying to you, dear friend, is that God wants you to get your eyes off of the waves. He wants you to put aside how you feel about things and simply listen to His voice. Faith always looks foolish to those who walk by sight. The will of God looks fearful to those who are led by the flesh, but to those who walk by faith, to those who are led by the Spirit, the will of God is not hard to find nor to follow. It all depends on where you are looking.

Chapter 6

How to recognize God's voice

Seventeen, that's how old I was when we had a pastor from the eastern side of Kansas come and preach a revival in our church in Hoxie. I had grown up in a church planter's home, I had seen God work in our family and through my dad's ministry, but quite frankly I didn't have any desire to go into ministry myself. We had always been provided for, but I wanted more. I wanted money. I decided that I would be a lawyer and I had every intention of remaining in church. I even thought about how much I would be able to help missionaries once I was rich. I thought about how I could fund my parent's ministry and make things so much easier for them. That is why, during that particular revival, I was struggling so much. I could not really tell you what the messages were. It wasn't that there was a certain statement that troubled me. It was just a nagging ache in my spirit that kept asking me if I would be willing to give up being a lawyer and having money to be a preacher. I didn't want to, and I was so miserable! I told my dad, one day, that we should have an all-night prayer meeting for revival, but I had an ulterior motive. I thought that I might just convince God to let me just give Him offerings instead of my life. Remember though, that God will have obedience and not sacrifice.

It was about 1:00 in the morning when I finally gave

into the will of God. I remember telling my dad, "We might as well go on home, God isn't going to let me off the hook." He said, "For what?" I replied, "He is calling me to preach and I might as well go ahead and surrender." It wasn't written in the sky, there was no miracle that caught my attention, it was the still small voice of the Holy Ghost of God that was speaking to me that night. I was not all that familiar with His voice at that time, but I have become so with time. I don't mean to say that there is an audible voice of God, but rather the direction of His speaking within your spirit that is so distinct that it might was well be audible. Just as we saw in the last chapter in Romans 8:16, "The Spirit itself beareth witness with our spirit, that we are the children of God:" The voice of God is Him bearing witness with our spirit of His presence and His will.

How did Peter, John, Paul and all of the other figures of the New Testament know the specific will of God for their lives? The same way that we can. First, they were obedient to the good will of God, they did the will of God for all people. This included studying the scriptures that they had and spending time with God in prayer. If you are going to learn how to discern the voice of God, then you must come to the place that prayer is more than an occasional practice. Prayer should be more than a monolog; it is intended by God to be a dialog. We pour out our heart to Him and we seek His direction and response. It is important as such, that in prayer we ask God questions and wait for His answers.

We are told in the Lord's model prayer that we are to

ask for God's will to be done on earth as it is in heaven. What does that mean? It means that we are to submit ourselves to the will of God on this earth so that He can work through us here as He would work there. This isn't about praying that others will do the will of God. It is about praying that God would reveal His will to you and submitting yourself to Him to do it. That being the case, it would behoove us to ask Him what His will is and listen to learn it. God, what do you want me to do today? Lord, who do you want me to minister to? Father, how do you want me to witness today? You see it is through prayer and the careful study of God's Word that you will learn to hear His voice.

At first it will be cautiously, meaning that you will be somewhat uncertain of what His voice sounds like. But after time, you will come to know and love His voice. You will long to hear from Him daily! Jesus said in John 10:27, "My sheep hear my voice, and I know them, and they follow me:" That isn't just a metaphor, He wants to speak to you daily. He is calling and teaching, but far too many believers are not listening. We are told in 1 John 2:27 "But the anointing which ye have received of him abideth in you, and ye need not that any man teach you: but as the same anointing teacheth you of all things, and is truth, and is no lie, and even as it hath taught you, ye shall abide in him." The Holy Ghost wants to be your teacher in all things, He wants to speak to you and guide you; but you must learn to listen to His voice.

As I go to God's Word daily, I am not reading for

distance (trying to get through a certain number of chapters). I used to do that, but now I have learned that the Lord has a message for me in His precious book. So instead, I read to hear from Him. I read until the Holy Spirit causes something to stand out to me. Sometimes it is a verse I had never noticed before, sometimes it is a very familiar verse or phrase. It may even be the general context of a passage that catches my attention and I stop to meditate on it. It doesn't matter if it was a single verse or an entire book, I stop reading when my attention is arrested by the Holy Ghost. I spend time meditating on it and praying about it. I used to wonder how it was that old-time men of God would record that they spent hours in prayer, when I could hardly spend minutes. Then I discovered that they often prayed through scripture, asking God to open His Word to them, asking Him questions and simply sitting in silence for sums of time, waiting for His answers.

He directs to other passages; He illuminates and gives understanding. This is exactly what Paul is speaking of in 1 Corinthians 2:7-16, "But we speak the wisdom of God in a mystery, even the hidden wisdom, which God ordained before the world unto our glory: Which none of the princes of this world knew: for had they known it, they would not have crucified the Lord of glory. But as it is written, Eye hath not seen, nor ear heard, neither have entered into the heart of man, the things which God hath prepared for them that love him. But God hath revealed them unto us by his Spirit: for the Spirit searcheth all things, yea, the deep things of God. For what man knoweth the things of a man, save the spirit of man which is in him? even so the things of God knoweth no man, but the Spirit of God. Now we have received, not the spirit of the world, but the spirit which is of God; that we might know the things that are freely given to us of God. Which things also we speak, not in the words which man's wisdom teacheth, but which the Holy Ghost teacheth; comparing spiritual things with spiritual. But the natural man receiveth not the things of the Spirit of God: for they are foolishness unto him: neither can he know them, because they are spiritually discerned. But he that is spiritual judgeth all things, yet he himself is judged of no man. For who hath known the mind of the Lord, that he may instruct him? But we have the mind of Christ."

As a believer, you have the indwelling Spirit of God., He not only seals you to the day of redemption, but He speaks to your spirit and teaches you, illuminating His Word and directing your path according to His will. The problem is that many, if not most, believers have never taken the time to become familiar with His voice. They are listening to so many voices that fill the air claiming to speak for Him, when they could be going directly to Him. In seeking to all the voices that say they speak for God, they are drawn to the ones that match up with their own feelings and desires rather than with His Word, far too often. This is why cults and schism abound. This is why people are drawn away after teachers, having itching ears and follow vain men into doctrines of devils. Paul warns the believers in Corinth about following personalities in 1 Corinthians 1:12-13, "Now this I say, that every one of you saith, I am of Paul; and I of Apollos; and I of Cephas; and I of Christ. Is Christ divided? was Paul crucified for you? or were ye baptized in the name of Paul?"

When a person has not learned to hear from God themselves, they start seeking for someone to follow who they think has. We are warned in 2 Corinthians 11:13-15, "For such are false apostles, deceitful workers, transforming themselves into the apostles of Christ. And no marvel; for Satan himself is transformed into an angel of light. Therefore it is no great thing if his ministers also be transformed as the ministers of righteousness; whose end shall be according to their works." This is why Paul said that the believers at Berea were more noble, because they did not even take Paul's words as truth without first searching the scriptures to be sure they were so. They wanted to hear from God Himself without the middleman. That should be the desire of every believer.

Chapter 7

Discerning God's will

Knowing how to recognize God's voice is a very important thing, and equally important is knowing what to do about it. We are given some direction concerning this by Paul in Ephesians.

Ephesians 5:8-17 says "For ye were sometimes darkness, but now are ye light in the Lord: walk as children of light: (For the fruit of the Spirit is in all goodness and righteousness and truth;) Proving what is acceptable unto the Lord. And have no fellowship with the unfruitful works of darkness, but rather reprove them. For it is a shame even to speak of those things which are done of them in secret. But all things that are reproved are made manifest by the light: for whatsoever doth make manifest is light. Wherefore he saith, Awake thou that sleepest, and arise from the dead, and Christ shall give thee light. See then that ye walk circumspectly, not as fools, but as wise, Redeeming the time, because the days are evil. Wherefore be ye not unwise, but understanding what the will of the Lord is."

As we have already mentioned, if we are to discern God's will, we must be walking with Him in truth. You cannot walk in the flesh and the darkness and prove what is acceptable to God. You cannot be in fellowship with the flesh and those walking in it and follow the will of God at the same time. Don't be unwise, if you are to discern the will of God in your life, you must be living a pure life and remove the influences of the flesh from you, otherwise, you will be subject to the deceitful lusts spoken of in Ephesians 4:22.

I have found that when I am walking in the Spirit, the voice of God has been confirmed in three distinct ways. First, the direction of God's will is always in line with the clear teaching of His Word. Someone once told me that the will of God will never lead you contrary to the Word of God. It should go without saying, that since the Word of God is forever settled in heaven, He would not be directing us to contradict it. Therefore, it is so important to study the Word and know it. How can you understand what the will of the Lord is, if you don't have scripture to compare it to? God would not lead you to quit going to church or to go to a church that is not teaching truth since He has told us not to forsake the assembling of ourselves together and warned us of the necessity of doctrinal purity. God would not lead you to marry an unbeliever since He has specifically told us not to be unequally yoked together with unbelievers.

You see, if we have questions about the specific will of God for our lives, we must first consider the specific direction of the Word of God. This alone will often rule out things that fall outside of God's will. It is quite telling that often, when people have come to tell me of decisions that they have made, very often they don't want to hear what the Bible says about it because they have decided to do it anyway. The truths and principles of God's Word do not matter to them. However, if you are wanting to be certain that you remain in the perfect will of God, the Word of God should be of supreme importance to you! You should be seeking direction on what the Bible has to say about the area that you are considering. I believe that the Word of God speaks about every area of life that we will face. It may not speak of specific brands or colors in that way, but the principles of the Scripture will give us guidance to make wise decisions within the will of God.

The second guide that I have found to be important to determining the will of God is whether it is in accordance with how we see the Holy Spirit direct others in the Bible. What I mean here is that we never see anyone in the New Testament saying, "God, if this is your will, then let this happen." We do see people taking time for prayer and fasting, we see people searching the scripture, we see people receiving godly counsel, but not asking God to act like a trained monkey and do a trick for us. When people come tell me that they know God's will, I always ask them how did they confirm that it was the will of God? Is it in line with how the Holy Ghost has spoken to others? That matters. I once had a man come to my office who had been living in sin for years. He sat on my couch and said, "Four weeks ago I got my life right with God and everything is what it ought to be now. Two weeks ago I started asking God if He wanted me to stay as a member of this church and He hasn't said anything to me at all about that. So I am taking that as God's will that He wants me to leave the church." I said, "So you asked God a question and He hasn't answered you yet, so you are going to make a decision to do something based upon God's silence?" He said, "Yes, I am". Can I tell you that is not how the Holy Ghost leads? First of all, if God told you to do something already, such as join a church, then why would you ask Him if He still wanted you to do what He had already told you to do? Secondly, God's silence is not His direction. God's will is not found in the unknown of your mind. There is no indication anywhere in the Bible of the Holy Spirit revealing His will by not giving direction.

The third guide that I have found is that God's will is confirmed by the spiritual authorities He has set in our lives. God leads through authority, that is completely clear in scripture. Hebrews 13:17 is clear when it says, "Obey them that have the rule over you, and submit yourselves: for they watch for your souls, as they that must give account, that they may do it with joy, and not with grief: for that is unprofitable for you."

In the spring of 2004, as we were traveling in evangelism, we drove through The Dalles, Oregon. As we drove through, my wife said, "This would be a great place to start a church. Even if the people are not nice, the scenery is great." I told her that I would never start a church anywhere because of the scenery and God would have to really give us a sign if He wanted us to go there. We weren't even talking at that point about starting a church. Forty miles down the road, we stopped at Multnomah Falls and looked around. Before leaving, we stopped in the bathroom and on our way out, my wife stopped in front of a sign that was eight foot tall and four foot wide that said, "All roads lead to The Dalles", she said, "Well, that's a sign." A few days later, we started talking about if it might be God's will for us to start a church and we began to pray for God to give us direction. We looked at several cities and continued to pray, but we could not get The Dalles off of our hearts. Finally we went to look at the city. As we were walking through downtown, a preacher friend called me and asked what I was doing. I told him we were spending the day looking around The Dalles. We had not told anyone about our praying concerning God's will, but he blurted out, "Brother Carter I grew up in The Dalles and ever since I got saved, I have been praying for God to send someone to start a church there."

We began to pray and fast more earnestly as we sought God's will and we were very confident after a few weeks that God was directing us to this work. I told my wife, though, that if it is God's will, He will also lay it on the heart of our pastor since it is churches that start churches and not just individuals. We prayed for several more weeks and were scheduled to be back in our home church for a meeting that August. One day, while we were back, I asked my pastor if I could talk to him. I shared my heart about what I believed to be God's direction and I was prepared to hear him say that he disagreed. We had been seeing great fruit in evangelism and I knew that my pastor was not quick to receive change. To my astonishment, he said, "Brother Carter, a few months ago the Lord told me that you would be starting a church and I have been praying that He would show you where He wanted you to go." I have never had a time in my life where God's direction was not confirmed by my spiritual authorities. I have had times when I went against the direction of my spiritual authorities, thinking I knew the will of God and they didn't, only to find problems and the absence of God's presence.

I have had people quote Acts 5:29 to me many times "Then Peter and the other apostles answered and said, We ought to obey God rather than men." This verse seems to be a favorite concerning disobeying the counsel of spiritual authorities. And taken out of context to fit our desires it seems to work, just like that all-time favorite Philippians 4:13, I can do all things through a verse taken out of context. Acts 5:29 is speaking about secular authorities commanding us to stop preaching the gospel, not spiritual authorities giving us caution and leadership. Proverbs 21:1 says, "The king's heart is in the hand of the LORD, as the rivers of water: he turneth it whithersoever he will." God can change the heart of leadership when He is giving direction. I have never found it wise to move forward with what I believed the will of God to be until God moved the heart of my spiritual leadership. I have found that I can get ahead of God far too many times and I needed that leadership to pace my progress so that I was in the right timing of God.

In following these three guides, I have found that the voice of God is available to every believer and He will not only speak, but He will guide our timing by speaking to those who He has set over us as well. It is wonderful when you hear from God in your spirit, and it is amazing to know His will in your life and to do it according to the direction of His Word. Knowing the perfect will of God and walking with the voice of His direction is one of the best things a believer can ever experience.

"Wherefore let them that suffer according to the will of God commit the keeping of their souls to him in well doing, as unto a faithful Creator."

1 Peter 4:19

Chapter 8

Distinguishing between a burden and a call

Romans 9:1-5 "I say the truth in Christ, I lie not, my conscience also bearing me witness in the Holy Ghost, That I have great heaviness and continual sorrow in my heart. For I could wish that myself were accursed from Christ for my brethren, my kinsmen according to the flesh: Who are Israelites; to whom pertaineth the adoption, and the glory, and the covenants, and the giving of the law, and the service of God, and the promises; Whose are the fathers, and of whom as concerning the flesh Christ came, who is over all, God blessed for ever. Amen."

A while back, I was watching a show on television, which may not be the best way to start this chapter. However, I was watching a show and a commercial came on which showed children in distress. It talked about how needy they were and the hardships they faced. It showed them in an unfinished room, which was their home or school, and I'm sure that you have seen things like this before as well. The goal, of course, of the commercial was to tug at the heart strings and create a burden in your heart for these poor, needy, destitute children so that you will pick up the phone and add a monthly charge to your account. For only 99 cents a day, you can feed or cloth or provide water and school for a needy child. Now there is nothing wrong with helping people. We have people in our church who have been helped by these programs and I have nothing against such help. My point is that these commercials are intended to create a burden within your heart to cause you to act to alleviate a problem that you have seen.

As you look at the passage in Romans 9, we see Paul begin a discourse that is focused on the idea that he feels he might have been a little hard on the Jews and that they might be withdrawing from his teaching because of the way he has reprimanded them on their views on the law and on grace. This passage begins with Paul sharing the burden that is on his heart and he extends this as he details the national election of the nation of Israel. This chapter has nothing to do with individual election or salvation, it is specifically a confirmation to the Jews that they were supposed to be the people of God but they cast off the promise that was given by God and rejected the truth and thus have lost the blessings God intended them to have.

As he begins, however, he opens up his heart and shows them the burden that he has for them. It is much like what I do as a pastor when I preach on something that I know will be hard to hear. I spend a good deal of time reminding my church that I love them and I am not telling them things because I am angry or because they are evil. But rather, because of my love for them, I am telling them what they need to know from God's Word. That is how Paul begins here and is, in essence, saying, "I want you to see my heart and understand why I am sharing these things with you and why I am saying it in this fashion."

If you go back through Romans, the book was actually written with the Jewish believer in Rome in mind. Though he was writing to the whole church in Rome, the Jewish believers were the focus because of the air of self-importance that they had in looking down on the Gentile believers there. This problem was creating a schism in the church in Rome and Paul was trying to bring out the point that faith is not about your linage or what you used to be or how you used to practice. We are all equal at the foot of the cross and we must come to the place that we recognize that. He is trying to bring back to their remembrance then, that the gospel did come to the Jew first and, in doing so, he opens up his heart and shows the depth of his burden for Israel.

In considering this passage, I realized that there is an important truth that can be seen here in the burden of Paul. In our church, we currently have a number of families that have surrendered for full-time ministry. I am frequently asked by these men, "How do I know the difference between a burden and a call? How do I know if it is me that wants to do something or if it is God directing me to do something?" As we look at this burden that Paul exposes and consider what we know of Paul concerning the call of God on his life, realize that Paul is not talking here about the call of God on his life. He is talking about the burden on his heart. I want to consider, for a bit then, what this passage tells us about a burden and how to identify it.

First, it seems clear that a burden is from you, it is from your heart. A burden is when you see a need in a group of people, and you have a concern for them. Such as I mentioned earlier, a burden about the plight of suffering children or a group of people who are suffering. There is no shortage of people in our world who are suffering. You don't have to look very far to find people who are experiencing poverty and pain. Quite honestly, war, poverty and the ravages of sin are so prevalent that all you have to do is turn on the news today and you will find someone who is suffering. If you see that and it never burdens you, then you probably are too calloused to the suffering of others around you. The needs of others should create a burden and we should certainly be tender toward others. A burden, however, is not a call; it is my feelings toward others. Paul describes a burden here that puts a personal weight on your heart. He says there, in Romans 9, that he had a great heaviness. If you look up the word heaviness you will find the definition given is burden. Thinking about the needs of the Jews gave Paul a great weight of burden for them.

Paul goes on to say that it was a continual sorrow. A burden may cause a lifetime of grief in your heart. The phrase continual sorrow means a constant grieving in his heart, he was grieved for the Jews. Paul had grown up as a Jew, he had been educated in the Jewish traditions and doctrine and he had a zeal for these things. His zeal was so great that he was willing, before his salvation, to dedicate his entire life to putting down anything that would hinder the tradition and doctrine that he held so dearly. Once Paul got saved, he looked at his own people and saw them lost in traditions, lost in the false narrative that had rejected the word of God. Often, we talk about the Jews in the New Testament and consider them as idolizing the law, but it was really the traditions that they had elevated above the Word of God that was their downfall. The synagogue was not under the law, those were created after the destruction of the temple. If someone came into church and said that he thought we ought to learn how to practice like they did in Bible times and they went to a Jewish synagogue to learn, they would not find anything like what the Old Testament worship was. They created substitutes for the keeping of tradition and they elevated traditions and the teaching of rabbis over the Word of God. Paul saw his people and how lost they were in their traditions and in that, he saw his own former self and that he had once been blind to the gospel as well. This was a grief to him to see his own people in that same situation.

In verse 3, he goes on to say that he could wish himself accursed from Christ for His kinsman. A burden will cause you to be willing to trade places with those you love. I have a desire for people to be saved but what Paul is talking about is beyond simply a desire for people to be saved. Paul is saying here that he would go to hell for Israel if he could. This is a very heavy burden on his heart.

As I have examined the Bible and tried to understand

the difference between a burden and a call, I find that everywhere I have looked I found that a burden is to a people, but not necessarily to a work. You can love a people so much that you do a work, but the work will not ease the burden. A burden is a wonderful thing in its right place. It's good when God gives us a burden for what He has called us to do, but a burden that takes the place of a call can hurt us.

Let me explain that by considering what a calling is. It says in Acts 16:6-10, "Now when they had gone throughout Phrygia and the region of Galatia, and were forbidden of the Holy Ghost to preach the word in Asia, After they were come to Mysia, they assayed to go into Bithynia: but the Spirit suffered them not. And they passing by Mysia came down to Troas. And a vision appeared to Paul in the night; There stood a man of Macedonia, and prayed him, saying, Come over into Macedonia, and help us. And after he had seen the vision, immediately we endeavoured to go into Macedonia, assuredly gathering that the Lord had called us for to preach the gospel unto them."

Notice in this passage that the call was not simply to go to Macedonia and the call was not to the people of Macedonia, rather the call was to preach the gospel unto them. Do you see the difference here between the call of God to Paul in Acts 16 and the burden of Paul in Romans 9? In Romans 9, the burden was about the people, the situation of the people and their lost condition was heavy on the heart of Paul. But here the call was not just to a people but to a work. The call to Abraham was similar in Hebrews 11:8, "By faith

Abraham, when he was called to go out into a place which he should after receive for an inheritance, obeyed; and he went out, not knowing whither he went." Every place we see a call, there is an instruction to a work.

Paul never says he had a burden for the Macedonians; he says God called him to preach the gospel to them. Paul never said that he would be willing to be accursed for their sakes, yet he was called to go and preach the gospel there. God gave Paul a work to do in Macedonia. But when speaking of his own people, he never says that God called him to reach the Jews. He says he had a burden for the Jews. A call is from God, a burden is from you. Lamentations 3:51 says, "Mine eye affecteth mine heart because of all the daughters of my city." The reality is that when I am called by God to go do a work, as I see the need, a burden may develop in my heart. However, a burden in my heart does not equal a call from God.

A call from God will be directed by the Holy Spirit. This is a blessing! It isn't your work; it is His work. He is the one that will do it through you. When you follow a burden the work rests upon your shoulders, when you follow a call the Holy Ghost of God will do the work through you. A call will be directed by the Holy Spirit as to location (where), time (when), the duration (how long) to stay and the work (what to do). We see all these things in Acts 16, go here and don't go there, stay here and go now, do this when you get there. A call may be open-ended as it was with Abraham and you won't know when you will end when you start, but you certainly will know when you have arrived as Abraham did. You see, there is a great contrast between a burden and a call in the scriptures.

Think about the contrast between a burden and a call in the Bible with me for a minute. Moses as a young man had a burden for his people; as an old man he had a calling to his people. The results were very different. When following his burden, Moses killed a man and as a result spent the next forty years of his life in hiding. When following his calling as an eighty year-old man, he led his people out of bondage.

In Ezra and Nehemiah, we see two men who had a great burden but there is a unique thing about them. In both cases, their burdens were for a work. God called them then to the work that they had a burden to do. As you look at Nehemiah, you see that before his calling, Nehemiah was burdened about the walls of Jerusalem and how they were broken down. His burden for the work caused him to pray and he didn't do anything else about it until he received a call from God to go. Ezra was burdened that the worship in the temple had ceased and he talked to God about it until God gave him a call to go and rebuild the temple. In both cases, they had a burden for the work and God gave them a call to the work. It's kind of like what the Bible says in 1Timothy 3:1, "This is a true saying, If a man desire the office of a bishop, he desireth a good work." In this case, it is clear that the issue is not a burden toward a particular people but toward the need for men to take up the work of the ministry. When a man is burdened for that and begins to pray for God to call men to the work, it is often that God will call that man. You would be wrong to jump ahead of the call of God, however. Just as Nehemiah and Ezra prayed and waited for the call of God to go, so should every man who desires the office of a bishop wait until there is a call to go. When God calls, He also provides and equips but when you follow a burden you will often be unprepared and pay for it.

In the New Testament, we see many burdens. One such can be seen in Christ Himself as He stood, looked at Jerusalem and wept and said in Mat 23:37 "O Jerusalem, Jerusalem, thou that killest the prophets, and stonest them which are sent unto thee, how often would I have gathered thy children together, even as a hen gathereth her chickens under her wings, and ye would not!" Jesus was burdened for them, but He did not allow His burden to overtake His call. His call was to come and give His life as a substitute for our salvation, not to gather Jerusalem together to Himself.

The maniac, when he was freed from the demonic possession, had a burden to follow Christ but Jesus told him no. Instead, Jesus instructed him in Luke 8:39, "Return to thine own house, and shew how great things God hath done unto thee. And he went his way, and published throughout the whole city how great things Jesus had done unto him." The maniac did not follow his burden, rather he did according to the call of Christ on his life and just a few chapters later we read about multitudes of people turning to Christ in that region. The burden may have appeased him, but it would not have accomplished God's will in his life.

Think about Paul himself. Paul had a burden for the Jews but a calling to plant churches among the Gentiles. Now, as long as Paul followed his calling, we not only see him enduring persecution and tribulation, but we also see multitudes being saved and churches being established all over the region. God was doing a great work through Paul and while he was being stoned God, protected him and would raise him back up and he would go on to the next city. Over and again, as Paul obeyed the call of God, a great work was done through him. I am not trying to disparage Paul here, but at a certain point Paul allowed his burden to overtake his call and he took on him a Jewish vow. Some would say that this was okay and even try to say that it was within God's will for Paul. I cannot agree with this because Paul rebuked Peter for following Jewish traditions and then took a Jewish vow, shaved his head and went to the temple. As he was going, the Bible tells us specifically that men under the influence of the Holy Spirit told him not to go (Acts 21:10-11), but Paul went anyway because he had a burden. The result of Paul following his burden was that he was in prison the rest of his life and ultimately died. I am not saying that God didn't use him in prison, he penned much of our New Testament in prison, but he could have penned the same as a free man while starting many other churches. We will never know how much more Paul could have accomplished for God if he had not gone to Jerusalem. We know that he was intending to go to Spain and preach there, but we never see that accomplished in the Scriptures.

A burden is a wonderful thing in its proper, place but when you allow a burden to take the place of the call of God it becomes dangerous. The danger in following a burden, instead of a call, is that a burden will consume you, where a call will fulfil you. God will often give you the needed burden where you follow His call, but He does not often issue a call to follow a burden when it is for a people group as opposed to His work. So how do you tell the difference? Let's consider that for a minute before we end this thought.

First, weigh the factors. Is there a clear direction to a work from God or is it a burden for a people? Let me give you a few examples from our own missionaries in our church. Bro. Grissom felt that God wanted him to go back to England. He had a great burden for the Gypsies in the North because he had been there before and reached some of them. He didn't have a burden for the south of England, but we went and looked at Plymouth. I asked him to spend a few days in Plymouth and make sure he knew the call of God. During that time I was preaching in a church a few hours away and there happened to be a woman who had driven over there to attend a service at a Bible preaching church that very night. I gave her information to the Grissoms and they met with her. She told them that there was no one preaching the Gospel in Plymouth and begged them to come and preach the gospel on the streets there. Bro. Grissom heard the call of God much as Paul did for Macedonia. While his burden was for a people, his call was to a work.

A few years ago, we went to Italy with the Keisters. They had a heavy burden for Rome, and I asked them to pray and see what God wanted, rather than just follow their burden. In all the places we visited, they would say no, this isn't the place. Then one Sunday we were in Regio Amelia. Brother Keister preached there that Sunday and an adult man trusted Christ. We went to Bologna, which is only an hour and a half away, and while we were there they said, God wants us to come here and start a church. By the time we got to Rome their burden for it was behind them; their call had already been established by God.

In my own life, I can look back on decisions I have made based upon a burden and the results were disastrous. I can also take you to places where I heard the distinct call of God to a work. I heard God's call when we started our first work in northwest Kansas. God did a mighty work there. I followed a burden when we started our second work and it nearly put us out of the ministry. By God's grace, we found our way back into His will and after a time of training, I was obedient to the direction of my pastor to go do evangelism work for a year and then I again heard God's distinct call to start a church in Oregon. We did what God called us to do and we saw God do miracles. That is not an exaggeration. In January of 2008, while doing my devotions one morning, God called me to go back to pastor Beth Haven Baptist Church in Oklahoma City. I didn't have a burden for Oklahoma City, I didn't even have a desire to move back to Oklahoma City. I prayed about God's direction for several days and when I told my wife about it, she cried for several days. When we got married, she told me that she would live anywhere in the world except Oklahoma City. I knew that God called me, but I knew that the timing was not yet right because my pastor was still there. I waited on God's timing and in September of that year, I was called to be the pastor. We followed the call and in time God gave us a burden. If I would have stayed in Oregon because of a burden, I would have been out of God's will.

Is there a clear direction from God or is it just something on your heart? Has God clearly spoken to you about it? Are you seeking Him about it or trying to convince Him? It's ok to desire the work of God, but remember, when you allow a burden for a people to cloud your vision of the direction of God you will likely get in trouble. God is not ambiguous when He calls, you will know it.

God's call is to a work, at a place, for a time, and you should be very cautious not to allow a burden to take its place. A burden is a very poor substitute for the call of God.

“And be not conformed to this world: but be ye transformed by the renewing of your mind, that ye may prove what is that good, and acceptable, and perfect, will of God.”

Romans 12:2

Chapter 9

What knowing God's will does for us

Knowing God's will in your life is not only an amazing thing, it gives you a confidence to move forward as a believer like nothing else. In addition to much deep doctrinal and personal truth, the book of Colossians provides us with an incredible explanation of the power of knowing the will of God.

Colossians 1:9-17 says "For this cause we also, since the day we heard it, do not cease to pray for you, and to desire that ye might be filled with the knowledge of his will in all wisdom and spiritual understanding; That ye might walk worthy of the Lord unto all pleasing, being fruitful in every good work, and increasing in the knowledge of God; Strengthened with all might, according to his glorious power, unto all patience and longsuffering with joyfulness; Giving thanks unto the Father, which hath made us meet to be partakers of the inheritance of the saints in light: Who hath delivered us from the power of darkness, and hath translated us into the kingdom of his dear Son: In whom we have redemption through his blood, even the forgiveness of sins: Who is the image of the invisible God, the firstborn of every creature: For by him were all things created, that are in heaven, and that are in earth, visible and invisible, whether they be thrones, or dominions, or principalities, or powers: all things were created by him, and for him: And he is before all things, and by him all things consist."

Here, in this passage, we see no less than eleven powerful things that knowing God's will does for us. The first thing that we notice here is that knowing God's will changes our walk. In verse 10 it says, "that ye might walk worthy of the Lord unto all pleasing". If you are not walking in God's will, you will not be pleasing to Him. There is little doubt that walking contrary to God's will is displeasing to Him, but possibly more of an issue for many is simply making the decisions of life without ever seeking to know the will of God. There is a school of thought that God's will is just a smorgasbord of the possibilities we can take. This idea is that God doesn't have a perfect will for your life, and you can just pick the best of your options presumably using Bible principle. This idea seems to be contradicted by what Paul says in verse nine concerning his prayer for the believers in Colossi, that they would "be filled with the knowledge of His will in all wisdom and spiritual understanding". This would indicate that there is a more to the will of God than just making good choices or even just principled choices. It says in 1 Corinthians 2:10, "But God hath revealed them unto us by his Spirit: for the Spirit searcheth all things, yea, the deep things of God." You and I can only search the things of our own hearts, but the Spirit of God searches things that only God knows. This means that the Holy Spirit has access to a wealth of knowledge and information that we don't have. If I am relying on my own reasoning to make decisions, I am only operating with part of the information. If, however, I am seeking the Spirit of God to guide me in His will, I have access to everything that I don't know as well. The will of God is to conform our walk so that we might be pleasing to God. You might remain in the good will of God by simply trying to make principled choices, but the perfect will of God requires a dependence upon the Holy Spirit and seeking the face of God in prayer in order to walk pleasing to Him.

Additionally, knowing God's will and acting upon it will cause you to become fruitful. Bearing fruit is the evidence of God working through you to accomplish His will. The fruit produced may be evidenced in His Spirit bringing out His character qualities in me such as Paul mentions in Galatians 5:22-23, "But the fruit of the Spirit is love, joy, peace, longsuffering, gentleness, goodness, faith, Meekness, temperance: against such there is no law." As we are submitted to the will of God, the Spirit of God produces this fruit in us so that others see Him working in our members. It is an awesome thing to be in tune with the Spirit of God to the point that you know that He is working through you in a manner that is beyond your own abilities. When His love is manifest, rather than your own, and His joy is overpowering the issues that you are facing, His peace is keeping your heart and mind and so on down the line. That isn't possible if you are not in His will.

Fruit can mean more than His characteristics in us. It can also be born out in our ministry to others as we reach others for Christ or minister the Word of God to them so that they grow closer to the Lord themselves. This fruit is born out in the lives of others. Paul spoke of the fruit that he was bearing as a missionary that would abound to the account of those who supported him. When you show someone to the saving knowledge of Jesus Christ or you disciple someone in the Word, you are bearing fruit. There are, no doubt, many ways in which a person who is doing the will of God in their service for the Lord bears fruit. I would submit that the person who cleans the church so that others can come and hear without distraction is bearing fruit in the lives of others. The person who watches the nursery so that others can be in services and hear the Word is bearing fruit in the lives of others because they are helping the Word of God to go forward and lives to be changed. If it is God's will for me to clean the church, watch the nursery, faithfully pray or any other act of obedience to the will of God then there is going to be some fruitfulness in my obedience to do His will.

The third thing that I see knowing the will of God does in us, is increasing our knowledge of Him. As I know His will and do it, I learn more about the Lord. In my personal experience, I have found trying to explain a scripture to someone at their door or in discipleship has caused me to have an understanding at times that eluded me before. As I was preaching recently, I made a statement that I had never considered in my study but after I made it, I was helped by the thought myself. My obedience to the will of God to preach and dependence on the Holy Spirit allowed God to teach me more about Him while I was doing what He asked me. If you think that you can learn everything there is to know about God in the study, then you are sadly mistaken. One of my favorite statements on a personal level comes from a dubious source. Yogi Berra once said, "In theory there is no difference between theory and practice. In practice there is." I have found that many things that people thought they knew, because they reasoned it out, didn't actually work in practice. There are things about the Lord that you must learn firsthand by doing. You can speak all day about depending on the Lord but when you are faced with a problem, theory matters far less than the experience of knowing how God has provided before. God doesn't want you to just be an armchair theologian; He wants you to have skin in the game and learn firsthand about Him in a way that exceeds the platitudes of theory. Down in the dirt of doing His will, you will learn about Him in a whole new way.

Knowing the will of God will also make you stronger. Our text says it this way, "Strengthened with all might, according to his glorious power." When you know the will of God, there is a strengthening that comes to our spirit that causes you to be able to go beyond your own strength. Countless times I have experienced thinking that I could not go on, but because I knew the will of God, it gave me a strength that I would not have had on my own. When the circumstances are against you, knowing the will of God will strengthen you. When your flesh is weak, knowing the will of God will strengthen you. Think of all the times that Paul was stoned and left for dead or shipwrecked and all but lost. What strength do you suppose it was that caused him to stand up again or to hold on when he was in the deep? It was not a strength that originated in his own body; it was the supernatural strength provided by the knowledge of the will of God that his work was not yet done. I suppose that the reason many quit is because they are depending on their own strength rather than that of the Lord. Throughout the Bible we see the strength of God move men beyond what they could do on their own and accomplish the impossible for God. Knowing God's will in your life can allow you to do the same.

What does this strength look like in particular? It might look to others like a supernatural patience such as Paul speaks of in our text. The patience to continue when others quit comes from a strength beyond us. Some of my greatest heroes are those who, although others have told them to give up, have continued to plow the field they were called with the gospel. I cannot know God's perfect will for you, but I do know that if you are convinced that you are in the perfect will of God, you will have the patience to continue when others would have left long ago. I want to mention that the perfect will of God may be to stay in the same hard field for a lifetime, but it might also be to go somewhere for a few hours. I know that we can often be judgmental about people who we think should have left sooner and people who we think didn't stay long enough, but it isn't my job to know God's perfect timing for the lives of others. Adoniram Judson stayed in Burma despite not seeing much fruit but he has fruit that remains there until this day. I have a friend, who is a national pastor in the Philippines, that was led to the Lord along with four other pre-teen boys by a missionary who stayed for just one month. All four of those boys are pastoring churches now and have great fruit for the Lord. Was it God's will for him to be there for that month? Of course it was, but some might say imagine what he could have done if he had stayed longer. The reality is that he went on to have a very fruitful ministry in another country as well. We are warned in the scriptures not to judge another man's servant. My point, here, is that if your field is hard and you know it is God's will to remain, then knowing His will can give you the strength to patiently endure.

Strength might also look like longsuffering with joyfulness in our lives, as indicated in our text. Longsuffering is just what it sounds like, it is suffering long. But here it says that when we are strengthened by the will of God, we will suffer with a good attitude and even be joyful in the midst of it. If we are in the will of God, the suffering that would cause others to become angry and bitter can be used to make us sweeter for the Lord. The theme of the book of 1 Peter is how to respond to suffering. Consider the following verses found in 1 Peter 2:19-21 as an example of this attribute in Christ that should also be in us, "For this is thankworthy, if a man for conscience toward God endure grief, suffering wrongfully. For what glory is it, if, when ye be buffeted for your faults, ye shall take it patiently? but if, when ye do well, and suffer for it, ye take it patiently, this is acceptable with God. For even hereunto were ye called: because Christ also suffered for us, leaving us an example, that ye should follow his steps:" Jesus was longsuffering throughout His life, setting an example for us to follow. Have you suffered as He did? The truth is that we so often hit moment of suffering and turn into accusers of God or run for the hills. The reason for this is because we are walking in our own strength, rather than that of the Holy Spirit motivated by the knowledge of the will of God. Knowing the will of God also strengthens us to be longsuffering with joyfulness.

Paul goes on to tell us that knowing the will of God also will produce thanksgiving to the Father. I remember going through the time after we came to school at Beth Haven, when nothing was working as it should. The job hadn't transferred like they said it would and I couldn't find a good paying job. I was working in a warehouse and we were barely making it by. The budget didn't include paying the bills and eating. We got behind on the house payment and everything else. It was knowing God's will that gave us the strength, patience and longsuffering with joyfulness to continue going forward. It was during that time, that we saw God working in such unique ways and it caused thanksgiving in us for every little blessing. We had groceries show up on our doorstep, strangers give us money, and people in the church do things for us that I know they didn't have any idea we needed. Each time we would sit down with our children and share how great God is. Even though there was so much needed, we became thankful for each and every provision. After about six months, God had provided in such miraculous ways, and even though you could never do it by the numbers, somehow, God had provided, and we were all caught up. I went to work one morning, shortly after we had reached even again in our bills and they called a meeting to tell us that we would be losing our jobs in two months because the company was bought out. That day, as I went home, I was pretty low, but I kept thinking about how God had provided for us through all this time. As I pulled up to my house, there was a salesman for a local telephone company walking up to my door. He asked if I wanted to save money on my phone and I said I want to find a new job, are you hiring? Guess what, they were, within two weeks I had a new job and making five times what I had been. When I got my first paycheck we went to the store and bought an entire thanksgiving feast even though it was summertime. We fixed it all and gathered our children around the table to give thanks to God for all that He had done for us. God is so good! Being in His will causes you to see His provision and give thanks to His name.

In verse twelve of our text, we see that knowing God's will also provide a path to our reward. It says, "which hath made us meet to be partakers of the inheritance of the saints in light." What an awesome thought that God has an inheritance laid up in store for us. That inheritance, of course, consists of our place in heaven with Him, but it doesn't end there. There is a reward promised to everyone who is obedient in their service to the Lord. The rewards spoken of in the Bible such as the crown of life, the crown of rejoicing and others will be given at the Judgment Seat of Christ, or there will be an exposure of loss of reward because our motives were for self rather than for Christ. This is a judgment, not of our sins, but rather our works done or not done for Christ. This is not to determine our position in Christ, but rather our eternal place of reward in heaven. It is this eternal reward that motivated the apostles. They were serving earnestly so that they would have a greater opportunity to serve in the Kingdom. The idea that everyone in heaven will be equal in standing and position is not found in the Bible. There is a reward to be earned and an opportunity to serve in a greater way. Jesus said so in Matthew 20:20-23, "Then came to him the mother of Zebedee's children with her sons, worshipping him, and desiring a certain thing of him. And he said unto her, What wilt thou? She saith unto him, Grant that these my two sons may sit, the one on thy right hand, and the other on the left, in thy kingdom. But Jesus answered and said, Ye know not what ye ask. Are ye able to drink of the cup that I shall drink of, and to be baptized with the baptism that I am baptized with? They say unto him, We are able. And he saith unto them, Ye shall drink indeed of my cup, and be baptized with the baptism that I am baptized with: but to sit on my right hand, and on my left, is not mine to give, but it shall be given to them for whom it is prepared of my Father." I am astonished at the statement of some, that they don't want to serve for reward, as if they were somehow more holy and pious than Peter, James, John and Paul. God, in fact, calls us to serve for reward. Not indeed a reward for ourselves, but rather a reward that we can then give to Him when we bow before His throne. How horrible it will be to have nothing to give back to the Lord in that day. Walking in the will of God is the only path to earning reward.

Paul goes on to say in our text that we have been delivered from the power of darkness. I am so glad that this is true. When you got saved, you were delivered from the power of darkness. Satan no longer has power over you, unless you yield yourself to his influence in your life. Paul reminds us in Romans 6:15-16, "What then? shall we sin, because we are not under the law, but under grace? God forbid. Know ye not, that to whom ye yield yourselves servants to obey, his servants ye are to whom ye obey; whether of sin unto death, or of obedience unto righteousness?" Satan has no power over us and that is a truth that continues as long as we walk in the will of God. In the will of God, the power and protection of God is absolute; nothing can happen to the child of God in the will of God that is outside the control of God. Satan had no power to afflict Job without God's permission and the same is true for you. But, Satan did afflict Job you say, yes but not without the boundary set by God. Job was in trial in the will of God and thus was still always under the protecting hand of God. God's will for our lives is not always without suffering but it is always under His watchful care. If you venture out of God's will, you put yourself in the crosshairs of the devil and have left yourself vulnerable to his attacks without the protection of being in God's will. The devil has more respect for authority than some believers do. He knows that he cannot touch us without the permission of God, so being in the will of God we have nothing to fear from the devil. Though he may fight against what God has called us to do, he is already a defeated foe and God is greater!

Finally I want to consider that when we are in the will of God, it gives us authority to move forward. You see, if you are saved, you are in Christ. In Christ, we have redemption and forgiveness. What a glorious truth! Christ has all power. Let that sink in for a minute. It says in our text, "In whom we have redemption through his blood, even the forgiveness of sins: Who is the image of the invisible God, the firstborn of every creature: For by him were all things created, that are in heaven, and that are in earth, visible and invisible, whether they be thrones, or dominions, or principalities, or powers: all things were created by him, and for him: And he is before all things, and by him all things consist." Do you understand that there is nothing that exists that wasn't created by Christ, and there is nothing that continues to exist without His sustaining power. It says in Matthew 28:18, "And Jesus came and spake unto them, saying, All power is given unto me in heaven and in earth." Since He has all power, has created all things, sustains all things and all things are for His pleasure (Rev. 4:11), then it is safe to say that if I am doing His will, I have the authority to do whatever He has directed me to do. No one and nothing can stand in the way of someone doing the will of God. When the disciples were faced with authorities that tried to stop them, they had a very specific response. Acts 5:29 says "Then Peter and the other apostles answered and said, We ought to obey God rather than men." God's authority supersedes any authority of man. As a matter of fact, all human authority comes from God according to Romans 13:1, "Let every soul be subject unto the higher powers. For there is no power but of God: the powers that be are ordained of God."

Paul shows us such amazing blessings that come from knowing the will of God. If you haven't already realized the need that we have to search out His will then I hope you will see the blessings that you are missing and commit yourself to the pursuit of God's will in your life.

Chapter 10

Staying in God's will

There is a constant struggle in the mind between what I can do on my own and what I cannot do without the Lord. Jesus said in John 15:5 "I am the vine, ye are the branches: He that abideth in me, and I in him, the same bringeth forth much fruit: for without me ye can do nothing." If you are reading this book, you probably already believe this, but far too often we fail to live accordingly. We start off our day doing the things that we can and before we know it, we have reached a point that we realize we are in over our heads. There is a very good illustration of this in the scriptures.

Luke 2:41-49 "Now his parents went to Jerusalem every year at the feast of the passover. And when he was twelve years old, they went up to Jerusalem after the custom of the feast. And when they had fulfilled the days, as they returned, the child Jesus tarried behind in Jerusalem; and Joseph and his mother knew not of it. But they, supposing him to have been in the company, went a day's journey; and they sought him among their kinsfolk and acquaintance. And when they found him not, they turned back again to Jerusalem, seeking him. And it came to pass, that after three days they found him in the temple, sitting in the midst of the doctors, both hearing them, and asking them questions. And all that heard him were astonished at his understanding and answers. And when they saw him, they were amazed: and his mother said unto him, Son, why hast thou thus dealt with us? behold, thy father and I have sought thee sorrowing. And he said unto them, How is it that ye sought me? wist ye not that I must be about my Father's business?"

Traveling in Christ's time was not only difficult but dangerous. The terrain leading up to Jerusalem was very rugged and provided many places that thieves could hide, as illustrated in the parable of the good Samaritan. For this reason, most people would travel in large groups. This was the case with Joseph and Mary. They were with a large group that was traveling together. They must have gotten up in the morning and as they were packing, saw Jesus around them. They probably saw Him wonder off, thinking that He was going to be with some other boys in the group. As they got busy it simply never crossed their mind that He would not have been somewhere in the group of their friends and family until they were at the end of an entire day's worth of traveling. They settled down at the end of that first day and expected Jesus would be coming back to the tent, they started looking around and asking their friends, was Jesus with you today? Did you see Him anywhere and what a shock when they finally discovered that He was not with their group at all. They just made the assumption that He was traveling along with them.

This is often an assumption that we make as well. We have our plans, we just get up and start moving forward. We don't mean to leave the presence of God or the will of God but we find ourselves at the end of the day, looking around and realizing that we have somehow left Jesus far behind us and now we are out here all alone.

Just as nothing is greater than being in the perfect will of God, nothing is more miserable than getting out of the will of God after you have known it. I often say to my church, "You don't have to decide to walk in the flesh, that is your natural state. All it takes to walk in the flesh is to fail to decide to walk in the Spirit." Staying in God's will is a constant decision. At any time, you could separate from the will of God by simply failing to choose Him and instead walking in the flesh.

The decision that we must make constantly, if we are going to stay in the will of God, is to live the gospel. What do I mean by saying, "live the gospel"? I mean that every choice, every temptation, every thought should be dealt with just as Paul says in 2 Corinthians 10:5, "Casting down imaginations, and every high thing that exalteth itself against the knowledge of God, and bringing into captivity every thought to the obedience of Christ;" I must bring every imagination and thought into obedience to Christ through the gospel. I must choose to die to my lusts and live to His resurrection over sin. I must choose to die to my fleshly impulses and live to His victorious power.

This is what Paul was speaking of when he penned Philippians 3:7-10, "But what things were gain to me, those I counted loss for Christ. Yea doubtless, and I count all things but loss for the excellency of the knowledge of Christ Jesus my Lord: for whom I have suffered the loss of all things, and do count them but dung, that I may win Christ, And be found in him, not having mine own righteousness, which is of the law, but that which is through the faith of Christ, the righteousness which is of God by faith: That I may know him, and the power of his resurrection, and the fellowship of his sufferings, being made conformable unto his death;" Living the gospel means that I consider this world as dung and His will as my very life and breath.

Paul said in, Galatians 2:20 "I am crucified with Christ: nevertheless I live; yet not I, but Christ liveth in me: and the life which I now live in the flesh I live by the faith of the Son of God, who loved me, and gave himself for me." Living the gospel means that it is not my life, but Christ's life in me. This is truly what God's will is for every believer. It isn't just where to work, what to drive, what to wear or listen. It is that every decision and every temptation should be taken to the cross of Christ and laid before Him and that we should die to ourselves and live to Him.

If you are serious about living in the will of God, this is what is required. Oh sure, you can live in the acceptable will of God without this, you can do mostly good things and have a mediocre Christian existence like this. But you can never live in the perfect will of God, you can never know the power of God, the closeness of His presence and, the distinctness of His voice like He wants you to, until you make that choice to live the gospel in every moment. Do you really want to know the will of God? Do you really want to stay in His perfect will? You can, and He wants you to as well. But you cannot accomplish it in the power of your flesh. It takes the power of the Holy Ghost within you and you yielded to Him in everything.

To be honest, that is a bit much for most people. We want just enough of God's will to make things go well for us but not enough to actually change us. We are much like the people in 2 Kings 17 who were brought to re-inhabit Samaria by the king of Assyria. Because they did not fear the Lord, He sent lions among them to kill them. The king of Assyria sent a priest to teach them the ways of the Lord and the Bible says in 2 Kings 17:28-33, "Then one of the priests whom they had carried away from Samaria came and dwelt in Bethel, and taught them how they should fear the LORD. Howbeit every nation made gods of their own and put them in the houses of the high places which the Samaritans had made, every nation in their cities wherein they dwelt. And the men of Babylon made Succothbenoth, and the men of Cuth made Nergal, and the men of Hamath made Ashima, And the Avites made Nibhaz and Tartak, and the Sepharvites burnt their children in fire to Adrammelech and Anammelech, the gods of Sepharvaim. So they feared the LORD, and made unto themselves of the lowest of them priests of the high places, which sacrificed for them in the houses of the high places. They feared the LORD, and served their own gods, after the manner of the nations whom they carried away from thence."

What an astonishing passage, they feared the Lord, and served their own gods. I fear that is where many who claim to be Christians are today. They fear the Lord because of judgments that might come, they fear the problems that rejecting Him could cause, but at the same time they continue to serve their own gods. They continue to serve their lusts and cravings from a wicked culture. They want enough of the will of God to keep the problems away, but not enough to actually change what they do.

Do you truly want the will of God? Do you truly want to know His voice and presence? If so, you can! He is not hiding from you. He wants you to know His will. It just requires that you separate yourself to Him, it requires that you draw nigh to Him. 2 Chronicles 7:14 is still true, "If my people, which are called by my name, shall humble themselves, and pray, and seek my face, and turn from their wicked ways; then will I hear from heaven, and will forgive their sin, and will heal their land." God will hear from you and God will speak to you, but you must do your part first and to continue in His will. You must live the gospel that you say you have believed.

Made in the USA
Monee, IL
02 June 2023